How to Hire:

A Recruitment Playbook for Rookie Recruiters, New Managers, and Growing Businesses

Pamela Shand

Copyright © 2020 by Pamela Shand.

All rights reserved. No part of this publication may be reproduced, distributed, or transmitted in any form or by any means, including photocopying, recording, or other electronic or mechanical methods, without the prior written permission of the publisher, except in the case of brief quotations embodied in critical reviews and certain other noncommercial uses permitted by copyright law.

ISBN: 9798691657214

Editors: Jen M. Watson/ Suzan Thompson
Cover Design: Link Creative

Acknowledgements

To the entrepreneur who puts their people first
To the hardworking recruiters and HR leaders working hard to push through the obstacles
To the outspoken leaders ready to shake up the status quo
To those on the front lines of hiring for their organizations

– This is for you.

Table of Contents

Introduction……………………………………….6
Why is hiring so difficult…………………………….7
Internal vs. External Challenges………………………..12

I. How Do I Know What I Need?………………………38
    (Organizational Requirements)

II. How Does The Public See You?……………………63
    (Employer Branding)

III. How Do I Know What's Out There?………………68
    (Market Research, Competition, & Compensation)

IV. How Do I Evaluate Applicants and Candidates?……………………………………..72
    (Launching the Search, Reviewing Resumes & Interviewing)

V. How Do I Leverage Technology?………………….92
    (Applicant Tracking Systems, Interviewing Software, and Mobile Devices)

VI. How Do I Manage My Candidates?………………..95
    (The Candidate Experience)

VII. How Do I Know What NOT To Say Or Ask?………………………………………………99
    (Employment Laws & Best Practices)

VIII. How Do I Welcome Someone Into The Company?..102
(Offers & Onboarding)

IX. How Do I Plan For The Future?......................105
(Training, Retention, & Succession Planning)

X. How Do I Put This All Together?....................107
(The Take-A-Ways & Do's and Don'ts of Hiring)

Conclusion……………………………………………119

References………………………………………….120

Introduction

The hiring process, if it's going to be successful, requires several different elements working at the same time.

Candidates have to understand who they are, the value they bring to the table, and the kind of organization that best fits their needs. They have to be ready, willing and able to sell themselves in an interview and put their best foot forward every day while on the job.
Leaders (you) have to be self-aware. You have to know what you can offer and what you cannot. You have to be real about what your challenges are and be open to all possibilities.

This book is called "How to Hire" for a reason. It helps to examine the struggles employers like you face every day and how to overcome them. It's about understanding how to navigate the market you're in, confront the things that hold you back, and identify the kind of talent you need. Recruitment is like matchmaking. When the right person is aligned with the right role, it's magic!

Every candidate is not going to be a match for you, and that's OK. It's not about getting every candidate to like you. It's about attracting the right kind of talent to your organization and your job.

Why is hiring so difficult?

A business is its people. That's a fact.

Your business isn't your processes, your social media presence, your technology, or how much revenue you generate. It's your people.

During my time in talent acquisition, I've heard the same from countless business owners. From small business names to Fortune 500 names, when asked about their secret to success, they all give credit to the same entity. They all say that their people are the reason they are where they are.

I couldn't agree with them more.

I've always believed that the business is its people, and I still do. The fact that you're reading this book shows that, on some level, you believe the same thing. Without strong talent, aligned to the same mission, vision, and values of your organization, your business is severely limited and your potential is capped.

Without question, the absolute best way to take your business to the next level is by hiring the right people. It is your people that make your company's vision a reality and bring your mission to life. Your people shape your company culture, and whether they (or you) realize it or not, act as your biggest brand ambassadors.

As an employer (recruiter, business owner or team lead), the last thing you want to do is dismiss how important each step of the hiring process is. You must pay special attention to how you're crafting job descriptions and sharing your job opportunity with the public. Be cognizant of how you're treating people and managing the process. Don't make the mistake of repeating toxic processes and habits. Make sure you can afford to offer competitive compensation. Each step is important, and when you forget that, when you neglect or mismanage the critical steps involved, you waste a ton of time and money. You will fail to attract the kind of talent you need and continue to entertain people who aren't a fit for your business. Eventually, you'll find that you're wasting time interviewing the wrong people and investing in talent that's not a fit for your brand; talent that will never give you the return you need. Instead of adding value, you have a staff that is costing you money, and if this continues, you'll become more and more frustrated watching turnover increase and your business decline.

It's a counterproductive cycle, which ultimately makes the distance between where you are and where you want to be greater. Make no mistake, recruitment is an investment. Without a sound strategy, that investment will not yield a positive return—and that's not good business.

This is where "How to Hire" comes in. I wrote this book for anyone who either needs to hire for the first time or has always struggled with hiring and feels like they can't figure it out. It can be a struggle to understand the true needs of a business, then identify, attract, and select the kind of talent you need.

When hiring, there is so much to consider—from finding someone you want to hire, the employment laws impacting how you hire, interview strategy, and welcoming your new employee into your team and the organization. Having a tool like this handy will help guide you through the key parts of the process. Don't be surprised if you have to refer to this more than once. Think of this as your textbook, instructional manual, reference guide, and overall source of both accountability and encouragement when it comes to hiring the kind of talent your business and your team need. It was created to show you how to manage hiring in a way that works for you. This book will inspire you to be more thoughtful, proactive, and creative in how you identify talent for your organization.

This is also where we get real about the internal and external challenges preventing you from hiring successfully. As we get further along, we'll take an honest look at hiring from top to bottom; this includes tackling organizational needs and employer branding, and it includes a look at how to complete your hire with successful onboarding. We'll cover some really important laws and best practices pertinent to your business. No matter the size of your company (business group or team), this will help you hire better.

I hope that as you go through each section, you will be challenged to take ownership of where you are as an employer. Acknowledge the opportunities for improvement, face the hard truths, and take corrective action if necessary.

Finally, in the midst of all of the instruction and guidance, this book will drive you to address both your internal and external struggles with hiring. It will help you recognize and push through these challenges—ultimately taking the first steps toward building a better, more successful business through effective recruitment.

Pay special attention to the Thought Challenges and Pro Tips along the way. Keep a notebook handy. I strongly recommend that you write down your thoughts as you go through this book. Take the space in this book if you need to. Use the margins—whatever you need.

Writing will help organize your thoughts and guide you through the rest of the process. It will help you understand and later articulate where your needs are, design a job description, and create end-to-end recruitment strategies that work.

Don't shy away from the process. Better hiring equals increased revenue for your business. Studies show that companies that put more effort into a better hiring process, generate more than three times the revenue of their competitors who are hiring haphazardly.

The tools and guidance here will help you fix what's wrong, and will help you to create something just right for your business.

It's time to learn how to hire.

Internal vs. External Challenges

Before we can discuss any solutions to your hiring challenges, we must get real about the problems and causes behind them.

While unemployment goes up and down, there are still a ton of people in the job market ready and willing to accept a great offer. Some people who have been in the job market for some time, aren't there because they're lazy or lack experience. They're just waiting for the right opportunity.

Some, while employed, are dissatisfied where they are and are waiting for a great leader to hire them. They're not desperate, have no problem waiting to be challenged, and are only excited by the opportunity to be a part of something great. They want to learn from a leader just like you. They want to add value and help you take your organization to new heights. As an employer, you have to know this. You have to know that there are people who would love to work with and for you. Think positively and carry that positivity into all parts of the process. Avoid going into this with a negative mindset, as it will only make things more arduous than they need to be.

People who are in the job market, regardless of who they are, want to work. Job seekers know how to

appreciate good opportunities and are generally grateful when one opens up to them. The majority of people that are applying to jobs and interviewing are doing so because they truly want the job.
With all of that said, we now have to ask the obvious question: If there are so many people out there who genuinely want to work, why are hiring leaders (business owners, managers, recruiters, HR managers, etc.) struggling to find the talent they so desperately need?

We have to address the possible answers to this question head-on.

There are several key reasons why business leaders and employers struggle to find the right people to fill their roles; these don't have as much to do with money or the current state of the job market as one might think.

Some challenges are external like the ever-changing market, trends, etc. Some are internal and quite personal. We'll discuss the external challenges in a moment.

First, we'll address the internal challenges—some you may be aware of, others you may not. Either way, we're going to explore them and start on the path to finding the solutions you need for your internal struggles. We don't have control over the external, but we can confront our internal challenges and overcome them through practice.

Internal Challenges

Believe it or not, some of your biggest challenges with hiring come from within. Many leaders struggle with hiring, not because the market is bad, but because they're dealing with internal struggles and biases they're unaware of.

For example, if you meet a candidate, and immediately before they've said a word, you look at their appearance, take note of their gender, or a visible disability, and decide that things aren't going to go well or you'd never hire them, you may have some biases you're unaware of.

If you have a job opening, post an ad on a website, and because you aren't flooded with resumes think there's something wrong with the market, you may have some learning to do.

It's impossible to cure what you're afraid to acknowledge; so, we're going to acknowledge some common internal employer challenges one by one and discuss ways to address them. Without this step, you'll continue to stand in your way, and all of the strategizing in the world won't fix your recruitment issues.

Lazy Recruitment Practices

One of the biggest mistakes employers make is underestimating how much effort goes into finding great talent. They rely on the "post and pray" approach, where they blast out all of their open jobs online, usually to job boards, hoping that this will solve all of their problems. This simply does not work as well as many hope it will. Many truly believe that all they have to do is post a job ad and people will run to apply. It doesn't work that way.

The truth is that the kind of talent you're hunting for doesn't spend as much time on job boards as you'd think. They're usually too busy with their current jobs or running their independent consulting firms. They don't have time to scroll through job boards. You have to pursue them. You're going to have to market your organization to them and not sit back waiting for them to pursue you. Doing that will keep your job open longer than it needs to be.

Finding the right person for your company or team takes work—real work! You're going to have to invest time, and maybe some money, to get this done. You're going to have to network, market your employer brand, get on social media, and connect with schools. You're going to have to put work into finding out where the people you need to hire are and what their priorities are in order to successfully recruit them.

Pro-Tip: As a recruiter, I've always felt that my #1 priority is to listen. As an employer, this needs to be your priority as well. Before you go into your spiel about your needs and how great your company is, ask your candidate what they're looking for and what led them to apply for that role. Allow your candidate to do most of the talking upfront, while you simply listen. Listen carefully to the things that motivate them and get a hold of what their priorities are. Then, when responding, connect the dots between what's important to them and your company. If they start to talk about their family and the proximity of your office to their home or child's school—allow that to guide you in your response. Talk to them about your business' family values.
Do you offer discounts with local daycare centers? Mention that. Do you allow your people to work remotely and take wellness days? Great! Mention that.

If they're talking about their career goals and ambitions, talk about success stories within your organization and how supportive you are when someone wants to progress to a new opportunity. Engage the candidate from the beginning by speaking to their needs.

It's tough finding good talent, so you have to be willing to do the work. If your entire recruitment strategy consists of a list of websites you post to, chances are you fell into lazy recruitment practices. Your target audience probably has no clue who you are, what your company is about, or that you're even hiring.

Put yourself in a job seeker's shoes. They spend hours perfecting their resumes, creating profiles on popular job search websites, following your company pages on social media, creating YouTube videos, practicing their interviewing skills, researching your organization, and setting up automated job alerts tailoring their application to each job, just to get a foot in the door.

Many feel like they're made to bend over backward to get the attention of the employer(s) they want. They approach this process knowing how competitive it is. You have to do the same.

The truth is that the job market is competitive for employers and job seekers alike. Making the effort to do the work and actively listen to your candidates will help you remain competitive.
If you expect to attract the perfect person to your job, you're going to have to break away from "post and pray."

A Lack of Imagination

Sometimes the perfect candidate for you doesn't

look like what you thought they would, and that's OK. There is no "perfect candidate" mold, and hiring isn't "one size fits all." Be open to the possibility that your perfect fit may not look like what you expected.

Years ago, I was managing recruitment for a very selective, hard-to-please hiring manager. He thought he needed someone with 10 years of experience, a complex mix of skill sets, Ivy League degree, and experience working with one of our major competitors. Does any of this sound familiar?

To many, this seems like a dream. For this business leader, it turned out to be his nightmare. All the Ivy League candidates he interviewed had egos that turned him off. Those from our competitors wanted more money than he could pay, and those with 10 years of experience wanted his job—not the job he was offering.

Soon after launching the search, my hiring manager was miserable. After weeks of searching, I got creative. I presented him with a recent graduate, young in their career, with five years of experience.

After some convincing, he agreed to interview the candidate and loved them! He hired them shortly after, and they had a long and progressive career within our organization. They were promoted twice and often received higher performance ratings than their counterparts.

Sometimes, as a manager, you have to train yourself to see the potential in someone. You may think that you need someone with 10 years of experience and an Ivy League education, when what you really need is someone with five years of experience, with lots of passion, problem-solving skills, and the right attitude combined with a desire to learn.

When you lack imagination, you close yourself off from the amazing talent that may be out there for you. Be open.

Pro Tip: When you're on the hunt for candidates, focus on soft skills—those things you can't teach or learn in a classroom. You can train the other stuff. Be willing to do that. Your processes and the systems you use can be learned on the job.

Think outside of the traditional boxes; you just might surprise yourself and find a diamond in the rough.

You Are Unaware Of Your Biases

If you've ever been turned off from a candidate because of the way they looked, their gender, how old or young you thought they were, how they dressed, where they went to school or where they lived—guess what, you are biased!

You're also guilty of violating several parts of the Civil Rights Act of 1964; but that's something we'll cover later on.

Have you ever round-filed (*thrown away) a resume because the name on it was difficult for you to pronounce?

Did you ever make a snap decision about who someone was because of the address on their resume? Perhaps you didn't approve of the neighborhood they lived in or assumed the commute would be too far for them.

While I won't be so quick to put a label on you, I will say this—if you felt even the tiniest twinge of guilt crawl up your spine when reading any of the questions above, you have got some serious soul searching to do.

These are all examples of discrimination and possible proof that it's your biases and level of ignorance keeping you from connecting with the candidate(s) of your dreams.

To be clear, declining a brilliant, well educated, talented candidate because you didn't like their hair, address, nationality, name, color of their shirt, or thought they were too young, is stupid. Not only is it stupid, it's also illegal and one of the main reasons you have such difficulty finding someone who actually wants to work for you.

Unrealistic Expectations

There is a belief that if there is a hiring need, all you need to do is list your qualifications and you will instantly meet someone who meets everything on your list. Then, all you'll have to do is interview them and hire them. In reality, it's much more complicated than that.

Your in-house recruiter, agency partner, or HR leader cannot place a list of skills in a hat and wave a magic wand to magically make a person appear.

Truthfully, if you have a good recruiter by your side, they will challenge your list of requirements and align them with what's available in the market. They will be honest with you about what is available to you based on your location, what you're offering, and what you're looking for.

Successful hiring takes hard work, strategy, and a bit of luck. It is definitely not magic. You have to understand this bigger picture, or you will continue to struggle.

Before jumping into the recruitment process, take some time to align your expectations with the market. We'll get into the HOW later on, but doing this will help you avoid a lot of the pitfalls many fall into. It will also ensure your success in finding the right kind of talent for your organization.

Champagne Taste and Beer Money

If you aren't familiar with this expression, it's a common one that speaks to someone who wants what they cannot afford. They want the best, the most expensive, the highest quality, but don't have the budget to afford it. Some have a similar mentality when trying to fill their jobs.

When hiring, the more you require in terms of education, years of experience, and quality of experience will increase the salary and/or benefits your candidate expects. I'm not telling you not to have standards—you ought to have standards, but be realistic about what you can afford and consider this before launching a search.

By the time one applies for the role or confirms the

interview, they know what they can expect to earn and it's impossible to hide this information from them. This is the information age. Job seekers have access to a ton of information that they once didn't. All one has to do is hop on the internet and they can find salary information for their desired job title, industry, location, and company.

It's not hard at all. They are informed.

They know what they're worth and are not going to accept less.

As an employer, you need to step it up here. I'm not saying that you need to throw the money at each candidate, but you should be paying market rate (or something seriously close to it). You want to make sure you can offer something else besides money like PTO, perks, and flexibility in work location and schedule, etc. There are a ton of vendors that can help you.

Once upon a time, I was managing recruitment for a mid-sized company with a tight budget. We struggled to compete with salary, so what did I do? I got creative. I identified and partnered with a vendor that allowed us to offer a ton of perks to our employees and their families, at no cost to us. I understood that people care about working for a company that can help improve theirs and their family's quality of life. This helped us make our existing employees' lives better, and made us more attractive to the candidates in the marketplace.

The moral to this story is simple; when entertaining candidates, make sure the compensation package is worth their while. If you're unable to meet with monetary needs, get creative. Understand the core values and needs of your target candidate, and be prepared to meet those needs or remain short-staffed.

Company Culture/Management Style

When was the last time you looked up your company online?

Are you aware of your score on popular employee feedback sites?

Do you know what the popular ones are? You should.

Your scores there are seen by everyone, and are generally accepted as truth by those researching your company. This information is public and shapes your reputation in the marketplace. Job seekers see these scores and receive it as an indication of how they will be treated if they agree to work for you.

While company culture and management style seem like internal matters, they easily become public by word of mouth, and by these popular feedback sites.

The fact of the matter is, how you treat people who currently work for you, greatly influences your ability to hire the kind of talent you need.

For many job seekers, how they're treated at work is as important as (or more important than) how much they make. Many will take a slight pay cut for an opportunity to work with a great boss and get away from a toxic environment.

What's important to remember is that this helps shape your reputation in the marketplace; companies with poor reputations will struggle to hire and retain good people.

No one wants to work for a company that doesn't treat its people fairly, has a bad reputation, or a weak employer brand.

Poor Customer Service/Candidate Experience

You may be the interviewer, but that doesn't mean that you're above your candidate.

Remember that interviews work both ways. Job seekers are interviewing other companies just like you're interviewing other candidates. It's just as important for you to do well in the interview as it is for your candidate.

You need to ask the right questions, provide helpful answers to the questions you're asked, have a good attitude, remember your manners, and communicate.

Why?

Because your candidate is also your customer. There's a possibility that they will purchase your products one day or send someone your way who can help you. Don't turn your nose up and think that you are in any way above them.

If you do that, you'll continue your struggle to find good talent because no one will want to work for you. Good news spreads fast but bad news spreads faster. Job seekers are more vocal now than ever about their experiences, and won't hesitate to use social media to share those experiences with the world.

What's shared about you will either help you or hurt you. It's your choice.

Indecisiveness

Some employers struggle because they're simply unable to make a decision. They want to see resume after resume, conduct interview after interview, and never actually make an offer to someone. If you find that you get lost in the process and often need to see just one more candidate, you may struggle with indecisiveness. If you've ever lost a candidate (or candidates) because it took you too long to come to a decision, this is an internal struggle you may be dealing with and are unaware of it.

You don't need to see a million resumes before you make a decision, but you do need to see the right ones. Before launching your search, make sure you're clear on what your needs are (we'll talk about this later on) and what your priorities are as an employer. Make sure you're only interviewing people that you truly believe have the potential, based on their resume, to meet those business needs. The better you manage your process, the less time you'll have to spend pouring over resumes you aren't truly interested in, and the less time you'll spend scheduling interviews out of desperation.

In addition to managing the process properly, it's important to be self-aware as you go through each step. If you find that it takes you too long to find candidates you like, you feel the need to repeat the same steps in the screening process, and often lose candidates, you may be struggling with indecisiveness.

Confusion

You know you need help and cannot continue to run your business this way, but aren't really sure of the kind of help you need. Because you aren't sure what you need, you spin your wheels meeting lots of different kinds of people, unsure about whether or not they'll meet your needs now or in the future.

Before jumping to advertise a hiring need, take a moment to get crystal clear about what your needs are, your goals, and what you can realistically offer. This is no time to speculate.

Your business is important, and so are the people you pay to help take it to the next level.

Over-hiring

Over-hiring happens when employers see that there is an abundance of talent in the marketplace, or when employers aren't clear when it comes to what their needs are.

When there is an abundance of available talent and people are struggling to find employment, this is what is known as an "employers' market." It is one where the employer has an unfair advantage. In this type of market, individuals are well educated, diligent, and desperate. Employers know they have lots to choose from, and as such, many take advantage. From your standpoint, this may seem like a good idea. It may seem like you're getting executive-level talent for an entry-level salary, but there's much more to it than that.

When someone accepts a job from a desperate place, they do so with one foot in and one foot out. That commitment is never fully there. This means that while they may accept your offer and lower level of compensation for a while, they will keep their options open. In a short amount of time—too soon for you to see a real return on your investment—they'll be on to their next opportunity, leaving you back at square one.

When employers aren't sure about what their needs are, they hire based on a fantasy checklist, instead of hiring the person who is the right fit for their organization. They hire someone from a competitor, who has an MBA and 10 years of experience because that's the kind of talent they think they should be hiring. While it sounds good to say that your new hire looks good on paper and has all of these accolades, this may not be what your company needs at the moment.

Instead of hiring from a fantasy list, focus on what your organization truly needs (we'll talk more about this in a minute) to succeed, and hire accordingly.

Fear of being "out"-ted

One of the main reasons you consistently struggle to hire the right person is fear. Not to be confused with over-hiring, this fear comes on because, deep down, you're afraid that if you hire someone who is too smart, too confident, too ambitious, too strong, etc., they'll eventually take your place. You're afraid they'll outsmart, outwork, outshine, and eventually outgrow you.

It is this fear that's keeping you from acquiring the kind of talent you and your business need. It is this kind of fear that's holding you back.

As an employer, you are a leader, and as a leader, it is your job to inspire, motivate, groom, and ultimately create more leaders. You want to hire someone who can eventually take your place; that way, you're free to progress to your next level. When you hold your employees back, you hold yourself back.

Release those insecurities and hire the best talent you can find.

Instead of being afraid of a candidate's ambition or intelligence, embrace it. Lee Iacocca once said, "I hire people brighter than me and get out of their way."

Allow your new hires to use their awesome abilities and bright ideas to push your organization forward. That's why you hired them!

Emotion

The hiring process is an emotional one, and anyone who tells you otherwise is either misinformed, lacks experience, or lying.
Despite all of the systems we have in place to put science behind recruitment, there is still (and as long as people are hiring people, will always be) an emotional component there.

This is not a bad thing.

You have to like who you're working with, right? Liking someone, building a relationship (even a business relationship) is partly emotional, and we have to get real about that.

The problem comes when emotion is the only decision-maker. It shouldn't be.

If you're rushing to make a hiring decision because you're desperate, feeling impatient, or you interviewed someone who made you laugh, you're setting yourself up for failure. If you're turning down every hopeful because you're upset that their predecessor is gone and wish they'd come back— you're never going to hire anyone. If your feedback focuses more on how your candidate made you feel instead of their experience, professional presence, and successful track record, you are probably making decisions based solely on emotion, and that's not good.

Alternatively, emotion can keep you from seeing that someone great is right in front of you, especially if their predecessor was someone you really liked and enjoyed working with. Sometimes when we build such great relationships with those we work with, it's hard to imagine working with anyone else. When someone moves on to another opportunity, we're happy for them, but can become so attached to the way it used to be, we're unable to move forward with hiring another person. You become stuck, and that's not good. Your business has to move forward, and for that to happen, you have to replace the position.

The decision you're making to offer someone a job is a business decision and should be treated as such. While emotion plays a part, you have to remember that you're hiring an employee—not your new best friend.

External Challenges

External challenges are the things outside of your control. These are things that just happen and you cannot do anything to stop them from happening.
They are very real and happen to everyone. Here we'll discuss some of the more common ones.

Geographical Challenges

This is a real struggle.
There are many employers who struggle to find talent in their immediate area. Maybe your business is based in a small town, maybe you're a small business owner surrounded by Fortune 500 level competition. Perhaps a nearby employer is offering benefits or pay that you're unable to compete with. This happens.

Perhaps you're based in an area where it's difficult to find skilled labor. This also happens and you are not alone.

Be encouraged and remember that quantity and quality are two very different things.
While you may not always have a large number of applicants, you can focus on attracting quality candidates by approaching your search differently.
We'll look at some great ways to do that in a bit.

Interest in your business or industry is down

The business world is in a constant state of flux and the job market is a reflection of that.
Trends, as well as demand, in the marketplace are constantly changing.
Majors and career choices that were popular today may not be in the future, and businesses and hiring leaders have to prepare for this.
Blaming the market for a lack of available talent is somewhat of a copout.

The options are the same here as with any other challenge. You can cower at the sight of it or rise up to meet it. Put some thought into why interest is declining and how you can pivot and rebound.

Perhaps your business is rooted in an industry that's no longer in-demand.
For example, if you owned a business that made CD's

and DVD's, you're going to experience challenges; but that's not just the employment market, it's your industry as a whole. As we move forward, we'll discuss different ways to approach recruitment, but before looking at recruitment strategies, you will want to evaluate the future of your business.

Unemployment Is Down

A decline in the unemployment rate is usually a good thing for job seekers—not so good for employers. It turns up the competition and means that there are fewer people out there applying to jobs.

While this is a challenge, it is not the end of the recruiting world. It's times like this when hiring leaders need to be creative, proactive, and persistent.

Think differently about how you can connect with the kind of people you may want to hire. If people aren't applying to your job, go out and look for them. Don't give up.

Later on, we'll talk about some of the ways business leaders in your position can be more proactive and launch a talent search when there doesn't seem to be any available talent. It won't be easy, but neither was building your career/business, and you did that. You can do this too.

Candidates aren't passing background tests (including drug screen).

While for some, this may seem unbelievable, it is the reality for many.

There are industries and entire companies that have either relaxed or eliminated background checks and drug screenings primarily because of this issue. There is a debate as to whether or not background checks or drug screenings are truly necessary.

Consider this, if Ban the Box (explained in detail later on) doesn't allow you to ask for prior conviction information on the application, is it right to perform a background check where this would be discovered, potentially opening the door for bias (remember that word?)?

Also, if recreational marijuana is either legal or decriminalized in most states, why would one perform a drug test and risk failing a candidate they like?
There is a ton of debate around this. Ultimately, the choice is up to the employer. It's up to you. You can revise your process or reconsider how you're sourcing your talent.

Realistically, the market is always changing. The popularity of certain career paths and majors is always shifting. The ways that we identify and evaluate talent have changed and continue to evolve. Employment laws are updated regularly and we're all challenged to keep up.

We know all of this, and it is up to innovative business leaders like you to be agile, always ready to adjust with the changing tide. I hope that this book will inspire you to rebel against what you've been taught and disrupt all status quos.

If you identified with any of the internal or external challenges we just looked at, even a little bit—grab a notebook, a pen, and get comfortable. We have lots to talk about.

Part I

How Do I Know What I Need?
(Organizational Requirements)

There is an African proverb that says: "If you want to go quickly, go alone. If you want to go far, go together."

This speaks to the power of collaboration. Realistically, you cannot do everything by yourself forever. It's only natural that eventually, you will want help. You're going to need help, and it's important to build a team or collaborate with others if you expect your business to grow and be competitive.
This is the easy part for employers to understand.

The difficult part is HOW.

You know that you're going to need good people to help run your organization, but what exactly does "good" look like for you? Don't look for a cookie-cutter answer to this question.

It doesn't exist. What you need to do is identify what's going to work for your organization or team. Then, you need to figure out the best way to attract, engage, recruit, and hire that person (or people). Simple... sort of.

Let's take a moment to explore what a "good candidate" might look like for different types of employers:

Example #1
Kelly launched her investment firm last year and things are picking up quickly. She needs help managing operations.
For her, "good" might look like someone with a degree in finance and thick skin. She may also want someone with experience working with a startup.

Example #2
If you were running a beauty empire, you may want someone with applicable licenses and experience in the world of cosmetology.

Examples #3
If you were running a retail store, you may want someone who is an expert in sales and knows how to make money and operate a POS system.

As you can see, what makes a candidate "strong" or "good," depends on many different things.

Initially, when one thinks about the kind of person they need to fill a hiring need they might immediately start to list surface qualifications like educational background, technical expertise or years of experience. The reality is that actual hiring decisions are based on much more. In addition to being a match for the requirements of your job, you also need to make sure they're someone you can envision yourself working with day by day. Whether you admit this to yourself or not, you're going to hire someone you like. This happens because the true answer to the question of what makes someone good for your organization stretches beyond easy choices like education, years of experience and industry.

When you extend that offer to someone, you're hiring a complete person, and a person is many things. Also, there is a difference between what someone has and who they are. A degree is what they have. Passionate, hardworking, and a pleasure to work with is who they are. The technical skills one learns in a classroom or a seminar, can be taught on the job if necessary. The natural abilities, personal values or personality traits one possesses, cannot be taught, making them quite valuable.

The person you hire will bring NEW skills, abilities, ideas and more to your organization. Something you don't currently have.

What kind of people will you need to get your team or your company where it needs to be?

Talent is everything in an organization and if you're unsure what you need (notice I said "need" and not "want" – there is a difference), you'll continue to make poor hiring decisions.

When thinking about what you need for your business, you have to ask yourself some key questions:

What are the goals for my team, my department, or my business?

The person (or people) you hire will help you meet or exceed your goals. This will shape how they do their job and determine how their success will be measured. Informed candidates will be curious about this information, so have it handy and be ready to share it. Having this helps an employee feel engaged and connected to the mission right away.
In order for this to happen, you have to know what those goals are.

What am I in need of that I do not currently have?

When hiring, it's important to remember that who you hire directly impacts how prosperous your organization will be. You want the talent you hire to add value.

You're in need of something you don't currently have and hope the person you hire will bring that new thing (knowledge, skills, technical expertise, etc.) into your organization. If you've decided to implement a new system that will improve your process, increase efficiency, etc., you'll want someone who either has experience using that system or a similar system, as that will be an asset to your organization.

You're not looking to hire your friend. Hiring isn't about doing anyone any favors. This is a major business decision. The person you hire needs to be the right fit for your organization. They need to fill a need that you have, which isn't being met by your current staff, systems, or processes.
Keep this in mind as we go forward.

What kind of person do I want to work with?

In addition to the job related skills, the person you hire will also impact your company's culture.
Your company's culture (also referred to as Organizational Culture) speaks to the personality of your company. Typically, company culture centers on things like the work environment (even if you don't have a physical office and all of your employees work from home, this is still something to consider), company mission, vision, value, ethics, expectations, and goals.

The person (or people) you hire, will have to be a fit for the company. They'll have to share your vision, align with your ethics, and be willing to help you meet your goals.

If this is your company's or team's first hire, I'd recommend figuring this out before you start to assemble a job description or evaluating candidates. Remember that when you hire, you're hiring an entire person, who will bring all of who they are to work. They bring their skills and expertise along with their values, expectations, and priorities. As you're going through the process with each person, you want to make sure that they're going to be a fit in terms of skillset and culture.

What will this hire mean to my organization in 1 year / 5 years / 10 years?

This is a really important question to ask yourself as you begin to shape your new position. For full-time, permanent hiring needs, you'll have to think carefully about this. Where do you see this person in the future of your organization? What is the vision for this role? Ambitious candidates will ask this question, and while no one can predict the future, they will expect there to be a vision. What that vision is, can vary. Some companies have lots of structure, with a clear path for each position. Some don't, but that doesn't mean someone cannot build a career with your organization. While there may not be a vertical ladder of progression in place, there are plenty of ways for one to grow and learn within an organization.

Show your candidates that you've put thought into how they can continue to progress and prosper with you as a manager.

What can I afford?

Unless you're recruiting volunteers who are happy to come in and work for free, this is a valid question.
The job market is a competitive one – not only for job seekers but also for those who plan on hiring them successfully. Your budget plays a major role in how you hire. It impacts the strategies available to you (technology, job ads, agencies, etc., all cost money) and the caliber of talent that will be available to you.

If budget constraints are a serious issue for you, you'll have to get creative. We'll discuss how to get creative with sourcing in a moment. For now, it's important that you know and acknowledge how much of an impact your budget will have here.

When it comes to compensation for your new hire, you'll want to think about what you can consistently afford. Adding to your staff also means having a plan to generate income to cover these new expenses including benefits, perks, and any pay increases one may expect in today's world. I want you to be hopeful, but also realistic. This is no small matter, and as an employer, you will be counted upon to have a strategy for this.

It's important you start thinking about this now. The last thing you want is to hire someone great, only to lose them a short while later because you can no longer afford them; they also have their bills, families, and financial priorities to think about. Remember, who you hire is a business decision. Before making any major business decision, it's expected that a strong leader counts the cost before moving forward and be aware of what's truly required.

Another great thing to consider is that compensation is many things. It is more than one's salary, overtime, pay raises, or bonuses. One's monetary earnings are a piece of the puzzle. Anything that an employee receives or is awarded in exchange for doing a job can be defined as compensation. This would be wages, but also benefits (health insurance, 401K plans, pension plans, company matches, etc.), equity in the company (i.e. stock options), PTO (paid time off) in the form of vacation, personal days, mental health days, sick time, and any other rewards received from an employer.

Do your research to determine how your budget compares to pay expectations. If you discover that you aren't able to offer as competitive a salary as you hoped, consider offering more on the benefits.

Your ability to be creative here will get you quite far. Speak to the priceless needs of your chosen candidate. Focus on what's important to them, then look at what you can realistically afford and proceed from there.

If they value more time with their families, add additional PTO.
Negotiate. Negotiate from a place of understanding and genuinely wanting to meet their needs.
Think about what you can consistently afford over an extended period of time.

Soft skills vs. Technical skills

"Hire character. Train skill." - Peter Schutz (former CEO, Porsche)

A human being is never just one thing. We are multifaceted, with lots to offer. The things that make someone a strong candidate aren't wrapped up in their formal education or years of experience with your largest competitor. What makes someone a strong candidate and culture fit for your organization is a set of skills called "soft skills." These are a blend of skills unique to the individual. These are things that are innate or developed over time. While many employers today invest in soft skills training, the most valuable of these are not things one can usually learn in a classroom.

Can you imagine trying to teach one how to have integrity or a winning attitude?

Can you teach someone how to have a strong work ethic?

It's impossible. While there are some who are able to put on the mask and pretend for a while, eventually the mask comes off. As time goes on and certain situations arise, you will see the individual for who they truly are. Keep your eyes open. When those character-revealing moments present themselves, don't dismiss them.

While habits can be developed, these natural skill sets are something that one has to possess, and as an employer, it's up to you to hire for what you cannot teach, and train where you can.

Let's examine the case below:

Jennifer is a new manager and needs to hire an assistant manager as soon as possible. She needs an additional pair of hands to handle the expected growth that's coming for her team. Her company is implementing some new systems and will need someone who can handle the rapid increase in volume. She interviews lots of people and it's down to the final two candidates. She likes them both and needs to pick one.

Nicholas has an MBA, with seven years of experience in finance. He's been in finance his entire career and possesses nearly every qualification in Jennifer's job ad.

Brenden has a BA, three years of experience in finance, and prior to finance, worked in restaurants for five years.

Jennifer knows she needs someone who can do the job and handle the challenges along the way. After much deliberation, she decides to hire Brenden. Why? Why would she hire someone with less education and fewer years of experience?

During Brenden's interview, he shared examples of how working in restaurants, mostly during busy times of the day and on weekends, taught him how to manage sudden increases in workflow. He learned how important it is to be prepared and have the answers for your customer before the question is asked. He learned how to think on his feet, handle pressure, and maintain a positive attitude no matter what. As he was sharing his experiences, Jennifer thought about how much she desperately needed this for her team. While the company had lots of people with MBAs and Ivy League educations, there weren't a lot of people with Brenden's passion and positivity. It was clear that he was someone her organization and her team needed.

Jennifer knew something that many hiring leaders do not – You can't get an MBA in Positivity (at least not yet).

What gave Brendan the advantage were his soft-skills. They made him a great culture fit and not just a technical skills match.

In his interview, he was able to demonstrate his value as a person, not just give a bulleted list of qualifications. While education and technical skills are fantastic and important, there was more to him. When Jennifer recognized that, she opened the door for Brendan to bring all of who he was to work. When he's hired, Brendan will bring not only his fantastic education and experience, but also that passion, positivity, good instincts, and decision-making skills he showed during his interview.

Someone like Brendan is more likely to disrupt and defy what exists and make it better.

He'll bring real value to Jennifer's business, be a benefit to the company culture, and be the kind of talent ambassador she needs.

Take some time to think about how you evaluate people. Do you find that you're so impressed with credentials that you overlook work ethic? What are the things that make a resume impressive to you?

Let's look at the following questions:

These will help you to understand what is needed for your business.

- What are the words that you'd use to describe the people in your organization?

Remember that a business is its people. It is your people that shape your company and team culture. Are your people kind and helpful or are they more aggressive, expecting every new hire to learn quickly and then either sink or swim? Both create unique company environments that won't be a fit for every applicant.

- How do I and those that work for me typically dress? Do you have a dress code?

How your employees choose to (or are encouraged to) dress sends a message about your company's culture. Most companies have a social media presence. Pick an organization and look them up on social media. If they have photos of their employees, pay special attention to how they're dressed. Acknowledge how the pictures you see make you feel and the impression it leaves with you. If you see a photo in which everyone is wearing suits vs. one where everyone is wearing jeans and a t-shirt, you will have very different impressions of that company's culture. Sounds small, but dress code (if you have one) makes a difference.

- o How do we as a company and/or as a team typically make decisions? Are we a "top-down" organization? Bottom-up?

The method used to make important decisions is very important in helping one understand your company culture. In a top-down organization, decisions are made at the senior level and shared to each tier of the organization. In a bottom-up organization, the reverse is true. Senior leaders look to their direct reports to tell them what's working, what isn't, and make recommendations on how to improve.

- o What are your organization's core values?

Your core values are those things that mean the most to your organization. If you haven't defined this yet for your organization, now may be a good time to start putting some thought to this. You're growing, and having a defined set of core values helps you effectively communicate your organization's personality and priorities. If integrity is a core value, each employee and business leader, from the mailroom to the boardroom, needs to model integrity every day. Think about how your organization currently operates or aspires to operate. Think about some words you'd use to describe the priorities of your organization. These will help you design your core values and hire talent that aligns with them.

- What are the global influences (cultural traditions, language, etc.) that shape how my company or team operates?

This can be a tough one for many to understand and explain; however, this is a very real part of the global business world we all work in, and shapes how many organizations function. For example, when I worked for a small company where our Founder and CEO was Italian, it was common to hear Italian spoken around the office, and we were all encouraged to eat throughout the day and have cannoli and espresso in the afternoon. Our head of finance along with many of our customers were native Spanish speakers, so it was common to hear Spanish spoken daily as well. When I worked for a company where my CEO was Jewish, it was common to hear certain expressions when something really good (or really bad) happened. Also, all of our catered lunches were Kosher, and the office closed early on Fridays to honor the Sabbath. These things were perfectly legal and not done to oppress anyone. They were a part of how the company operated. They were a part of our corporate culture.

In order for someone to be a great fit within your organization, they would have to understand this and be comfortable working in environments that looked this way.

- What is your mission statement and vision for the organization?

This is a really important question to ask yourself early on. Your mission and vision are the foundation for all that you do as an organization. They help frame your "why,"—your reason for being a team or company. This helps to communicate to the public who you are and what can be expected. It helps to effectively communicate your brand to the world. It's your standard. If you already have your mission and vision in place, use it to define your employer brand and apply it in your hiring practices. If you don't have a mission and/or vision statement, now would be the perfect time to get this in place. Not only does it make hiring easier, it makes things easier for your future hires. They'll be able to approach their roles with confidence, knowing from the onset what is expected and how to be successful.

- How would I describe the work style of the people that are most successful here?

- What about those least successful?

Think about the people you work with now, and the things that make them such strong employees. Think about some of the adjectives you'd use to describe them. If you look at a few of them, you'll see some commonalities among them. These commonalities should also align with the way you describe your company's culture.

Some are considered good employees because of their experience, but for many, it's the unique things they bring to the table without being asked. For example, you may have someone who comes in early to get a jump on the day. You may have someone who is great with building and managing relationships with key clients and customers, which is vital to your business.

Other employees may not be as strong as your top performers. Think about why there are people you're working with right now that may not be as strong as you would like them to be. Think about what skills they may be missing. Perhaps their shortcomings are skills related. If so, these are things you can train and hopefully improve. If it's a lack of motivation, work ethic, or something else, make a note of it. This will help you know what to avoid when designing your hiring strategy.

Whatever it is, make a list of these terms (good and bad) and keep them in mind when hiring. These adjectives along with the words you used to describe your company's culture will help you identify the kind of person/people you want to hire, as well as the kind you'll want to avoid.

- Do we make time for charity work or community service?

For many organizations, giving back is a major part of how they do business. It's common to see companies donating time and money to charities. They may also offer company matching donations as a part of their benefits packages or give their employees a day off specifically for community service. If you find that this is critical to your organization, you may find that having non-profit partnerships can be a fantastic way to connect with the kind of talent you're looking for.

Your honest answers to these questions will shape how you hire by forcing you to think about your company culture.

Have you ever interviewed someone, or been interviewed, and there was something 'off' about the conversation? There were no concerns around compensation, commute or experience, but there were other concerns that you just couldn't shake? These non-skill related concerns are usually associated with culture fit.

Here's an example: You're running a fast-paced company, valuing integrity, and embracing ambiguity, where everyone communicates by instant message.

You interview someone who lacks sense of urgency, moral fiber, and insists on conducting a meeting for everything. During the interview they demonstrated that they like to get every available detail prior to starting on an assignment and would be paralyzed without doing this. This person is clearly talented, educated, and experienced, but even with their impressive background, probably wouldn't be the best fit. Ultimately, they'd be unhappy working with you and you'd be unhappy working with them.

When you set out to hire someone, think about these things. Allow culture fit to shape your approach. You'll see a much better return on your investment (hiring is expensive) and you'll be much happier in the long run. Remember that it has to be a fit. You have to be a fit for them and they have to be a fit for you.

Now, speaking of you—let's shift the focus to you. After all, you are important here.

Keep in mind that as an employer, you're being evaluated as well. You're being researched on social media and employee feedback sites.

Your name is being typed into search engines.

Your candidates want to know who you are, who you worked for, and if they have anything in common with you. They're not just researching your organization, they're researching YOU, and they should.

Why? Because the interview is their opportunity to begin to develop a relationship with their potential boss or colleague—that's you.

Relationships are important. Many list having a good relationship with their boss as one of their primary job search requirements. I know that it's always been one of mine.

There's a popular saying I often hear in presentations and promoted on social media. It says that people join a good company but leave a bad boss. This is true. People care about who they work with and who they work for.

Who you are and how you lead, directly impacts your ability to successfully hire the kind of talent you need to take your business to the next level.

Take a moment to analyze who you are as a people leader.

Be honest.

If you know you have a lot to learn and aren't the best at managing people, it's OK to admit it as you go through the questions. Admitting it will help you do better.

This is not a time to fall into denial. It will only prolong the process, make hiring more difficult than it needs to be, and negatively impact future earnings.

Keep a pen and paper nearby as you go through the questions.

Take notes in the margins if you need to.
Do what you need to do in order to organize your thoughts. This book is for you. It's your playbook, your guide, and your resource. Use it as you need to.

- o What kinds of things do you need help with day to day?

- o Are these tasks that are simple yet time consuming?

- o Are these tasks complex and outside of my skillset?

- Is this a long term need requiring a full-time, permanent employee?

- Do I need temp staff for the next six months to two years just to get caught up?

- How would you describe your leadership style?

This could be derived from any or all of the items below:

- The internal/external process you follow when making major decisions.

- The way you typically communicate with others in business and in your personal life.

- The way others interpret your general attitude and reactions to things day to day. (Ex. Calm, cool and collected, passionate - caring deeply about every detail, coach/mentor, servant leader etc.)

- The way you react to your direct reports disagreeing with you. Does it make you uncomfortable or do you welcome it? What is your emotional reaction to this?

- Are there any special projects I need help with now? In the next six months to a year?

- Technical expertise: What systems do I use? What systems do I need for the future of my business?

If there is an industry specific system critical to your business, it will be important that the person you hire is either familiar with it or similar systems. If the systems you're using are homegrown, meaning that they were specifically created for your organization, you'll want to keep that in mind as well. The person you hire will have to be tech-savvy and able to learn new systems quickly.

- What does my company (or department's) growth plan look like?

- What is most difficult about working for my organization? For me?

- Candidates want the truth. That's a fact. A key mistake employers make is selling a candidate on the job. They're so focused on selling the role, they forsake honesty and miss the value of transparency.

  When you're hiring someone, you want them to respect the organization, you want them to feel a genuine connection with the role, and you want them to respect you.

  That won't happen if you sell them a dream

and things dramatically change once they're on board. Answering questions like these will force you to look inward, and that's a great thing. Remember that the hiring process works in both directions. You are interviewing and being interviewed. You extend the offer but need the candidate to accept it.

- How do I prioritize things and people? (Ex. Customers vs. employees. Some feel that if you care for the latter, they will care for the former. Others immediately put the customer first. Where you stand on this seemingly simple matter, speaks to your leadership style and what one can expect working with you.

- The way you behave when overwhelmed, when things get difficult at work, when there's a difficult customer to deal with, or unexpected challenge—Are you able to handle it well or do you freak out and lose it all over any and everyone around you?

Your responses to these questions will help you understand exactly the kind of talent you need. When you understand this, you can properly and fairly evaluate your candidates and make the best decision for your business. There is an added benefit here as well.

Going through these questions will help you to be

more self-aware. As an employer, this is important. The ability to hire successfully, hinges upon your ability to see yourself and your organization clearly.

Your success also hinges upon your ability to be open minded, creative, agile and persistent.

Thought Challenge: Avoid the "comfort zone" that's created when we hire someone who reminds us of ourselves. Your best hire may not have attended the school you did, they may not look like you or come from within your industry. Be open to the possibility that what you need won't necessarily fit into a familiar mold. Think about the kind of company you want to have and where you see it going. Remember that the person you hire will not only fulfill your needs as an employer, they will also bring new skills, experience, ideas, ways of thinking, and best practices into the organization. You want to hire for all of these things.

Part II

How does the public see you?
(Employer Brand)

When you think about your reputation, what the public expects from you and what separates you from others in the marketplace, you're thinking about your brand. When you think about this from an employment standpoint, you're now talking about your employer brand.

Take a moment and think about some of the well-known brands out there right now.

There are some companies that anyone would want to work for even if the pay was horrible. They just want to be associated with that company. They want to be able to have that name on their resume and say, "I work (or worked) there!"

They're proud to work where they do. They boldly tell everyone they know how great it is to work there, urging every friend, relative and/or college to submit an application.

These organizations have strong employer brands.

People flock to their tables at job fairs and apply to every job they post even when they aren't qualified. They just want to be associated with that employer's brand. Now, let's look at this from the opposite angle.

Imagine some of the companies with the worst reputation. They're out there and I'm sure you can name one or two. These are the companies that, no matter how much they offer, no one wants to work there—at least not for long.

These are the companies with toxic cultures, zero care for their people, high turnover, and terrible employee review scores. These are the companies with weak employer brands. These are the organizations that become laughing stocks in the recruitment world, and usually for good reason.

One's employer brand is something employers rarely think of as they grow, but it is extremely important, as it directly impacts ease of recruitment. Your employer brand is shaped by your reputation and helps to shape the way your company is viewed in the marketplace.

Established organizations spend years trying to design an employer brand strategy to share with the public.

To be clear, when I say "employer brand," I'm not

just talking about a cool hashtag or catchy slogan that you can use on social media. I'm talking about how you communicate your value and shape the expectations your candidates, new hires, and employees will have. I'm talking about the way you're viewed to those who may want to work for you one day.

Consider the following –
- How do people see you?
- What do job seekers and customers know about you?
- What do they expect from you?
- What's your employee value proposition?
- Do your employees/customers trust you?

Put the responses to these questions together. That's your brand. If your answer to many (or all) of these questions is, "I don't know," that's not good. You should be aware of your reputation and public image.

If the public at large sees you as an unjust employer who mistreats their employees, takes advantage of their customers, and doesn't pay their people well, you will continue to struggle. No one wants to work for someone like that. You need to have an employer brand that speaks to your core audience and helps you attract the kind of talent your organization needs.

Try this – Open up your favorite search engine and look yourself up online.

What do you see?

What presence do you have on popular job seeker/employee feedback sites?

Believe it or not, active and passive candidates (we'll tackle those terms in a bit) pay close attention to these ratings, and the companies with low ratings on these sites are more likely to struggle when trying to hire strong talent.

With unemployment as low as it is, the competition for talent is on and low employer scores won't help your chances one bit.

What about your story?

Is your story public?

Are people aware of where you're coming from as a company (or as a team), and have you done your best to truly engage your audience?

Do you tell your story when networking, posting to

social media, or interviewing candidates?

Make the history of your story, your mission, vision, and values public. Weave your message into all of your hiring materials and social media presence. Build campaigns around it to get the word out. Continually educate your staff on it and encourage them to share it.

Keep all of this in mind as you start to launch your search and engage candidates. If your scores are high, that's great. Feel free to expand on that when speaking to potential new hires. Talk about your people-focused programs and what you're doing as an organization to go from good to great!

If they're not so great, don't be afraid to tackle it head-on. Don't hide and don't try to avoid it. When asked about your challenges, be open and honest. Then admit that you're open to learning and moving forward with the right solutions. This shows that you care about your brand. You're aware of your challenges (remember, we talked earlier about being self-aware) and aren't afraid to tackle them head-on. This will help you attract the right kind of talent to your organization, despite your shortcomings.

Your employer brand is important.

This is critical for you to truly understand how to hire. Show that you care about it.

Part III

How Do I Know What's Out There?

(Market Research, Competition, & Compensation)

How you launch your search is the most important thing. In fact, it's everything!

This is not the time to be lazy, unrealistic or cheap. If you are, you will mess everything up and put your business in a really bad place. Pay attention to everything. Take the time to go over your job description. Make sure it's transparent and reflects the culture of your organization.

Remember when we talked earlier about communication style and culture fit?

Keep those principles in mind as you finalize your job descriptions.

Your job description needs to articulate your

employer brand and company culture. Let's be clear about one thing —the description is more than just a wish list of requirements.

If you put together your notes from the questions in Part 1, you'll have what you need to begin your job description, which honestly tells someone all about the kind of company and team they'd be joining, the kind of leader they'd be working with (you), the kind of work they'd be doing, how they're expected to do it, the tools necessary, and the vision around the role.

These are all the things today's job seekers care about and need to know early on.

As an employer, you have options around how you can launch your search. Those options largely depend on what the market looks like for you. Every available option won't work for every kind of position. We'll explore some of the more popular options in a bit. For now, put some thought into what the market looks like for you. Remember, you don't want to jump into your search with unrealistic expectations. Those who are most successful at hiring, understand their market and adjust their approach accordingly.

Let's look at some key questions below and get to know your market.

Your answers to the questions below are everything when launching your search. Again, this is YOUR textbook, reference guide, etc. If you need to take notes, write in the margins—by all means, do it!

Take a moment to ask yourself the questions below:

What does the talent pool look like for my industry, company size, and/or type of job I'm recruiting for?

Who are my business competitors?

What are they doing to attract talent?

How are people who do this kind of work being compensated? Hourly/salary?

Are bonuses common?

Am I prepared to compensate someone at that level? Can I compete?

Thought Challenge – Think about the essential job functions and things your future employee will need to do their job. Is this a sales role, where they'll be expected to travel? Will they be traveling locally? Internationally? For local travel, will they use their car? Are you prepared to reimburse them for gas, mileage, etc.? No one wants to feel as if they're paying for their job. The job is supposed to pay the employee, so if you're expecting them to

travel or utilize their own resources, you need to have an expense process or provide that method of transportation for them (i.e. a company car).

These are questions that any experienced job seeker (or one that knows how to look things up online) will ask. As an employer, having this sorted early on will help you understand the kind of candidate you can target. It will allow you to better engage potential candidates, confidently respond to questions, and avoid wasting your time or anyone else's.

Part IV

How Do I Evaluate Applicants and Candidates?

(Launching the Search, Reviewing Resumes & Interviewing)

Once you put your hiring need out there, you're going to attract applicants. It is from this pool of applicants you hope to find your candidate.

Active vs. Passive Candidates

When launching your search, the candidates you interact with will fit into one of two categories. They will either be active or passive. The Active Candidate is one that is actively looking for their next role. They are applying to jobs every day, and have accounts and profiles on all the major job boards and networking sites. The active candidate may or may not be employed. If employed, they're ready to resign for personal or professional reasons, or the job they have is at risk (job elimination, reduction in headcount, performance).

The point is, these are individuals who are ready to make a move right now.

This candidate applies online and will most likely make time to interview around your schedule, and respond to your offer quickly. They've already thought about it. Their mind was made up about your organization before they clicked, "Apply Now." They know they want to work for you, and are excited to receive your offer and begin working as quickly as possible.

The Passive Candidate is much different.

Whether employed or not, a passive candidate is happy just where they are. This is usually someone who you came across online, was referred to you, or someone you met and now have your eye on. They haven't applied and are in no rush to. They are content running their business or working for their current employer. They're happy with their pay, benefits, their commute, etc. As they see it, they have no real reason to leave their employer, or change anything they're doing; so, they can either take your offer or leave it.

This candidate will require more selling. You'll have to identify a need that your opportunity can fill in their lives. You may have to offer more than you originally expected and they may still reject your offer.

Many of today's in-demand candidates fit into this category. They aren't applicants. They aren't worried about updating a resume or sharpening their interview skills as much. They're accustomed to being pursued because of their reputation and strong relationships.

As difficult as it is to successfully recruit a passive candidate, many are drawn to them.

Why?

Because people who are taken are always more attractive.

There is a ton of debate around why passive candidates are more attractive to employers than active candidates, but there isn't one clear answer. When hiring, you want to be open to both. Either could be the type of candidate you need for your business. Remember that you're hiring the whole person, not just their current situation or status. Be open to finding the ideal candidate for you, whether they're active or passive.

Be proactive. Interview before you need to.

"I've been interviewing someone for five years. They have no idea. It's going really well." – Unknown (I have no clue who said this but I read it somewhere and thought it was fantastic!)

The exploratory (or informational) interview is your friend — MAKE TIME FOR THESE!

If you met someone at a networking event, through an alumni association, or have a neighbor with a talented child, schedule a follow up meeting.

Even if you don't have an opening at the moment, schedule an informational interview with them anyway.

This does a few things —

It creates what's called a candidate pipeline. The pipeline is another great friend to have in the hiring process. This is where you have people you can call on immediately when you do have an opening. Instead of posting a job or reaching out to an agency, you can pick up the phone and call that great person you met with last month and see if they're interested. This, in the long run, eases the stress of hiring, saving you time and money.

Did you recently fill a position and now have a stack of resumes from applicants with whom you never got a chance to meet?

Do any of them look good to you?

Create a shortlist and set up some quick calls to introduce yourself.

All it takes is 10-15 minutes to say, "Hi, I noticed that you applied to my job. While we elected to go with another candidate, I thought you had a great background and wanted to introduce myself. If you're ever interested in another opening with our company, give me a call. I'd love to keep in touch."

That's it.

That's all it takes to quickly connect with someone and start to build a real pipeline.

Advertise online - The internet is your friend

Job boards have come a long way since they were first introduced to employers. Originally, they were just a place to post your open job. Now, they can assist with pre-qualifying applicants through resume scanning tools and assessments, access to resume banks, connecting with "passive candidates" (people who aren't applying to jobs, but would still be interested), help schedule interviews, and act as resources for valuable market data.

If you're looking for people and wondering where they are, check social media. People are jumping on popular social media platforms every day, looking for old friends, new friends, current events, celebrity gossip, love, or something fun to do over the weekend. In recent years, as a way to cater to their millions of members, many social media sites have created job boards, where employers can find people they may want to hire. It makes sense! They already have millions of people interacting with one another through their websites and apps every day. Why not use it to look for a job as well?

Create a social media page or group to engage those interested in your company, industry, etc. If your company already has a strong social media presence, use that to connect with people you want to hire.

Join the Club

Do you have professional affiliations or memberships?

Yes? Great!

Use them.

Connecting with special networking organizations that cater to a specific audience is a great way to tap into the audience you need. If you look around, you will find specialty organizations catering to college/university alumni, specific vocations, diversity groups and/or interest groups. These are great because you can identify a target group of people who may satisfy some of your specialized needs. You can build valuable relationships, advertise your jobs directly and support events to connect with more people who fit the role(s) you need to fill.

Who do you know?

They say, "Good people know good people." I believe this to be true. If there is someone you respect and enjoy working with, it may be a good idea to tap into their network for your next great hire.

When advertising your job opening, don't put limits on your strategy. Share your opportunity with those in your immediate network. There may be someone in your community, your team, church, or someone connected to you via social media that's a perfect fit. Alternatively, those people in your immediate network may have someone in their networks that's a perfect fit for your role. Tap into the networks that are around you and solicit referrals.

If your current organization doesn't have a referral program, consider setting one up. Incentivize those with strong networks to refer talent to you and your organization.

Work the room.

Get out there and network.

How often do you attend networking events,

dinners, cocktail hours, etc.?

These events are crawling with talent. Your next great hire (or someone who knows your next great hire) could be in that room. Be open and ready to connect directly with people.

Recruitment is about people. The stronger your network, the easier recruitment and pipeline building will be, so when you have the opportunity to connect with people, do it!

Have someone else do the work for you.

These are popular for one very obvious reason — someone else does all the hard work for you while you sit back and receive résumés.

For a percentage fee, your agency recruiter will send you the kind of talent you need. This is a business, and their objective is to sell you a candidate they believe will work and seal the deal.

Keep in mind, your agency recruiter will focus on what you tell them you need for your business. This is why Part I is so important.

Without a clear understanding of what your needs are, you will waste time and money (agencies are not cheap) trying to identify the right person for your job.

Pro tip: Some employers make the mistake of using the words "applicant" and "candidate" interchangeably. Avoid doing this. They're not the same thing. An applicant is one who applies to your job. That's it. They may or may not have the skills you're looking for, but once they apply, they're an applicant. Once the applicant is selected for an interview, they become a candidate. They're now a contender and will remain a candidate until they become an employee.

You're going to have to review résumés and schedule interviews. Along with interviewing, you may want to incorporate some assessments into the process. This will not be an overnight process. There may be setbacks, and you may feel overwhelmed and exhausted at times. It's not easy evaluating people. It's not easy deciding who to interview and how to turn someone down. The ability to hire effectively is like a muscle, and this is where you develop it.

As you start to screen through resumes and schedule interviews, keep the words, "candidate experience," in mind each step of the way. There are many things that make up candidate experience; however, the ideal at the core of this is simple: treat your candidate like they're your customer because they are.

Be mindful of the details, like effective and timely

communication. Avoid last minute interview cancellations or reschedules. Remember that their time is just as valuable as your time.

If you require a candidate to travel for interviews, notify them of that in advance if possible. Give them time to prepare. You should also be able to cover those costs through direct purchase or reimbursement. If you're requiring them to travel, they shouldn't have to pay for it.

Remember that kindness is good business. Even if you're absolutely sure, the person you're interviewing won't be a fit, treat them well. Share feedback and hiring decisions in a clear, direct and respectful way.

While transparency is key, it's also important to apply wisdom and compliance with legal guidelines each step of the way.

Expect the unexpected

Great candidates can come from anywhere. You'll be surprised what you learn by sparking a conversation and getting to know someone.

As a recruiter, I've met great candidates in the unlikeliest of places.

True Story: I had car trouble one morning and decided to order car service to the office. As I got into the car, I noticed how clean and well-kept the car was. I complimented the driver on his car. After thanking me, he responded that he'd just returned from his second tour in Afghanistan. He decided to drive for Uber because it allowed him to spend time with his wife and daughter while looking for his perfect IT job. He grew up building computers with his older brother and wanted the kind of job where he could put his IT skills to use, but didn't want to spend his entire day cooped up in an office. At that time, it just so happened that I was recruiting for an IT role that required one to spend most of their time in the field on major projects, installing new technology and solving problems. While I hadn't seen a resume, I did get to know the person and knew he'd be a perfect fit for my job.

When I recruited for restaurants, I met this amazing young lady who was managing a local chain restaurant. Nothing impressive about that, but after getting to know her, I learned that her mom is a chef and she grew up in and around fine dining restaurants her entire life. Her current role kept money in her pocket while she finished school. If I went to a restaurant and loved the food or service, I'd slide my business card to the waiter or ask to meet the chef. Think outside the box!

Get in the habit of bringing your business cards with you everywhere you go. Avoid giving into any anti-social or shy tendencies you may have, and open yourself up to the possibilities that are out there.

Résumés, Screenings, and Interviewing

Remember those business needs you defined in Part I?

Go back to that.

Use that as the ruler and create a short list of those who "measure up."

Look for experience that speaks to what you need right now and what you need in the next year or two—especially if you want to hire people who will remain with you for a while and grow with the company. Remember that when you hire someone, you're making an investment. Like any other investment, you want to see a return, but you won't see that if the hiring process isn't managed properly.

PRO TIP: The Resume and the CV are not the same thing. Many employers use those words synonymously and they are actually opposites of one another. The CV encompasses one's entire work history while their resume is targeted and will highlight the strengths, soft skills, and accomplishments relevant to your job. It's important to know the difference and not request one when you really need the other.
Types of interviews

Phone vs. In Person vs. Video

Whether you choose to conduct phone interviews, in-person interviews, video interviews or a combination of all three, your priorities are the same. You want to establish a connection with your candidate. You want to get an understanding of their values, work style, and goals in order to assess culture fit. You want to confirm that they truly have the skills and abilities to be successful in the role. You want to confirm that this is going to work (i.e. do their salary requirements fall within the range of what you can realistically offer?). You also want to make the best use of your time. Put some thought into what method(s) will allow you to genuinely assess these key areas without pulling you away from being able to run your business.

Phone interviews are great in helping you to quickly assess whether or not someone meets the surface requirements of your role. For example, if you receive a resume that looks great but aren't sure they're a match on salary, you can ask them what they'd like to make. Use the phone interview to uncover any red flags that may arise. By the time you complete the phone interview, you want to feel that an in-person interview is a good idea. You should be excited about the opportunity of getting to know more about this great person with whom you just spoke.

PRO TIP: Avoid asking candidates what they're currently making. It doesn't align well with current trends in hiring, and depending on the state you're hiring in, can get you in serious trouble. We'll talk about that later on when we cover employment laws.

The in-person interview is a huge step. This is where you'll get the most out of the interview experience. You'll be able to spend quality time with your candidate, assessing attitude, and verbal and non-verbal communication.

PRO TIP: The in-person interview is also time consuming, which is why it usually isn't recommended for the first round. Consider conducting a phone interview as a first step. If you're still interested in learning more about the person, invite them in for an in person meeting.

Structured vs. Unstructured

Interviewing can be tricky. As an employer, you want to make sure you're making the right decision. Realistically, you can't interview everyone. Your time is limited for each interview, you don't want to waste time, but also know that it's important to get to know the person with whom you'll be working.

This means that you need to have a strategy that allows you to accomplish a few things:

Establish a rapport with your candidate. Doing this helps your candidate to relax. When candidates are relaxed, it's easier to get the responses you need to your interview questions.

Assess their strengths and areas for improvement. Focus on aligning their strengths with your job. It's easy to be carried away by the shiny objects (i.e. Ivy League degrees and club memberships), but these don't determine whether or not someone is a great fit for your job. Remember to focus on what's real.

Assess culture fit. Having that chemistry will allow you to assess fit and how well they'd get along with the rest of the team. Also, you want to get some insight into their values. If your company values integrity, you don't want to hire a pathological liar.

If this is your first time interviewing or hiring someone, you're in luck. We're going to cover trusted interviewing methods and how best to use them. We'll also cover their drawbacks, that way you'll know what's really going to work for you and your business.

For some, a structured interview with preset questions and scorecards works best. For others, they prefer a relaxed unstructured interview, where they can just have a conversation and get a feel for who they may end up working with. Many use a combination of the two, where they combine preset questions based on core competencies and core values mixed with small talk, and questions about the individual. This approach works for most businesses. It allows you to have a real conversation while still being able to make an intelligent decision on who you hire. Having some structure also helps with compliance and metrics tracking, which are critical in business operations. While there is an emotional component to hiring, it is a business decision, and you'll want to treat it that way.

1-on-1 vs. Panel Style

Many employers opt for a panel style interview, if they have the staff available, because there is a belief that it will save time. There is a belief that they can complete all necessary meetings simultaneously.

While this may be a time saver, it may or may not be the most helpful option for you or your candidate(s). Unless they're comfortable speaking in public or applying for a role that requires a ton of presentations, this option may cause more harm than good.

When conducting interviews, you want to get as much out of the experience as possible. If your candidate is intimidated by having to sit in front of four, five, or more people asking them questions one after the other — it can feel like sitting in front of a verbal firing squad. Some may feel an overwhelming amount of pressure, and find themselves unable to think clearly. This isn't good for you because it leaves your candidate unable to provide the kind of information you need. In addition to this, the candidate's experience isn't as good as it could and should be.

Sitting down with your candidate 1-on-1 allows you to have a genuine conversation and truly engage. The goal is to identify any synergies between your needs and the needs of the person with whom you're meeting. This person will add tremendous value, solve current and future problems, bring fresh ideas, and help take your organization to the next level. It's important that you create an interviewing plan that allows you to get to know them. The resume will reveal employment history and education. Here you want to dig deeper. Get a sense for their thinking ability, business acumen, values, and priorities. Focus on their valuable talents and those soft skills we talked about earlier.

The most important part of all this is follow up and decision-making. I know that hiring for many managers is scary. No one wants to invest in someone only to end up disappointed later on, but you will eventually have to hire someone. You have to make a decision or risk losing a great candidate to another opportunity. Remember that the interview process works both ways.

You have to communicate with your candidates. If the search is taking longer than expected, and you met someone you really like, tell them. Check in with them and keep those lines of communication wide open. Encourage them to reach out to you if they have questions.

Even if they aren't the one — let them know. Don't string them along because you're too focused on being nice. Trust me, they'd rather know the truth. They'd rather be turned down than ghosted.

Answering the candidate's questions

An interview is a balanced, professional conversation, where both sides have the opportunity to share their stories, brands, and what they can offer, hoping for alignment and a shared desire to work together.

In the beginning, you as the interviewer will be asking most of the questions. Before wrapping up, you'll want to give the candidate the opportunity to ask you some questions. This step has the potential to show you a few things:

- o This allows them to show you that they're genuinely interested in the opportunity by asking thought provoking questions about the role, the company, and you.

- It can show you how much research they've done before the interview to prepare.

- This can show you whether or not they were truly paying attention when you were speaking.

Always give your candidate the opportunity to ask questions. In addition to helping you identify the strongest candidate, it also helps you score major candidate experience points (we'll talk about candidate experience in a bit).

When researching an opportunity and interviewing, candidates simply want to know that your role and company will be a fit for them. You can expect their questions to revolve around this basic need.

Below are some question types you can expect to hear and should be prepared to answer:

- Tell me about your company's culture

- How will this role add value to the team and organization?

- What is the org/reporting structure like?

- What are your plans for the future of this

position?

- What does the compensation plan look like?

- Why is the role open/where did it come from?

- What are the challenges one can expect?

If you think back to what we discussed in previous chapters, you'll be well-equipped to respond to these questions and questions like these. Be honest and transparent with your candidate. Respect them enough to give them the information needed and allow them to make the best decision for themselves and their families.

Employee engagement is built long before one becomes an employee. It's built in the interview process. If they know that they can trust you in the interview, and the job is right for them, they'll be excited to work for you and put their best foot forward when they do.

Part V

How Do I Leverage Technology?
(Applicant Tracking Systems, Interview Software, and Mobile Devices)

We're living in a time when everything we do (for the most part) requires the use of technology. We use technology to communicate, get information, be entertained, go to school, shop, keep in touch with family overseas, and so much more. It would make sense that we're also using technology to hire and get hired.

Technology impacts each part of the hiring process and allows employers and candidates the ability to pull data; helping them understand how competitive they are, their negotiating power, and how well they're doing in the marketplace. Through technology, you have several tools like applicant tracking systems, mobile application tools, social media, reporting, and digital marketing tools all available to you.

Applicant tracking systems have been a part of how companies recruit for over a decade, and as they've grown and continue to grow, they show no signs of disappearing anytime soon. Employers use these to not only track applicant flow, but also build talent communities and employer branding efforts through social media and other digital integrations. While applicant tracking systems increase efficiency allowing you to sort through applications at a faster pace, it's important to remember that they aren't responsible for making hiring decisions. You are.

Most of us are using our mobile devices more than computers to search for and apply to jobs. Having a mobile application makes applying to jobs easier, which increases the amount of people willing to apply to your job. More applicants means more candidates and a stronger talent pipeline making future hiring even easier.

All of the popular social media sites now have either job boards or a way for companies to connect with talent. While there are paid services and tools available for purchase, these sites are mostly free to join, saving employers a ton in up-front costs. Use the popularity or social media to your advantage by instantly sharing your job openings with thousands of people free of cost.

So much of hiring, believe it or not, is data driven. Whether you're tracking how long it takes you to fill your open jobs, how much you can expect to pay in New York vs Los Angeles, or how to improve hiring efforts for key positions, data is critical to the hiring process. Properly leveraging technology in this way also helps with forecasting future hiring needs and planning for the years ahead.

Part VI

How Do I Manage My Candidates?

(The Candidate Experience)

The term 'candidate experience,' is used to define the way a candidate is treated as they're going through each stage of the hiring process. It's the perception of a potential employer that a job seeker is left with based on how the job search, application process, interview process, offer process, and onboarding are managed. Candidate experience is all about how you make your candidates feel.

This is important for a number of reasons.

1. Your candidates are also your customers. A popular case study on Virgin Media, shows that in 2015 the media giant attracted 27,000 applicants to their job openings, 18% of which were new customers. That same year, Virgin Media lost over 7,000 customers because they

happened to be candidates who we mistreated in the interview.

2. Poor candidate experience is expensive. Another example from the Virgin Media case study revealed that in 2017 it was discovered that poor candidate experience was costing Virgin Media $5M a year in lost revenue.

3. This directly impacts your employer brand, making it harder to hire. Candidates talk, and bad news spreads quickly. Once upon a time, job seekers went directly to a company's website and career page to get the information they needed. Today, candidate and employee feedback site and forums are more popular than ever before. When potential candidates are researching your organization, they're utilizing social media and third-party review sites to gain insight into your processes and what they can expect if they apply and engage in the process with your organization. If they're seeing feedback that is less than favorable, chances are they will not bother applying to your job.

It's a competitive market out there, and one sure way to get a leg up on your competition is to create a process that works and treats your candidates with respect. Your process should be easy. There shouldn't be any unnecessary hoops to jump through, and it should be just as easy to apply from one's mobile device as it is to apply from a computer. A candidate should not have to upload their resume then manually enter the exact same information they just uploaded.

This wastes the applicant's time and leaves them with a negative experience.

When scheduling interviews, give your candidate time to prepare. While I understand a sense of urgency, it's unrealistic to call a candidate for an interview taking place on the same day, and expect them to change their lives around to accommodate you. Your candidates had priorities before they came to you. They had their families, and their lives to think about. They may also be employed. Be as considerate as possible when requesting their time.

Thank them for making the time to meet with you. When they arrive in your office, treat them as if they were a guest in your home.

Did you know that if treated properly, even a rejected candidate can become a satisfied customer? Many retail outlets send rejected candidates coupons to shop at their stores as a consolation prize for interviewing.

Respect your candidates' time. If you have to cancel or reschedule, apologize. If you find that it's taking you longer than expected to come to a decision, check-in with your candidate(s) and update them. They will appreciate and respect how attentive you are. If you know that they are not the person for the job, don't delay in following up with them or avoid the conversation because it's uncomfortable. Candidates appreciate feedback. They want to know where they stand. Communicate with your candidate(s) and let them know that you won't be moving forward. Be professional. Be honest yet diplomatic.

Make it a point to stay up to date on changes to employment laws. Allow this to guide you in how you treat your candidates.

Treat your candidates and employees the way you'd want to be treated. Make sure you're considerate and respectful. Communicate with them throughout the process, making sure they're aware of where they stand. Discuss compensation more than once to make sure you're aligned, and reduce the chance of having an uncomfortable conversation at the end.

Be proactive about educating yourself on the laws and best practices that are in place, and remain compliant.

Part VII

How Do I Know What NOT To Say Or Ask?

(Employment Laws & Best Practices)

Employment Laws and well established best practices shape so much of what we do. You need to be familiar with these if you hope to have successful interviews and make solid hiring decisions.

Remember that we're in the information age.
Candidates are savvy and have access to a lot of the same information that you, your legal team, and HR leader(s) will have. They're comfortable looking things up, they'll be informed on these topics, and expect you to be as well. This means that it's important for you to be informed and prepared.

The Law: Employment Laws & Best Practices

Title VII of the Civil Rights Act of 1964

Title VII of the Civil Rights Act of 1964 makes discrimination on the basis of national origin, citizenship, age, marital status, disabilities, arrest record, military discharges, or personal information (such as height and weight) illegal. Unless there is a BFOQ exception*, any question that asks a candidate to reveal information about his or her national origin, citizenship, age, marital status, disabilities, arrest record, military discharges, or personal information is a violation of the Title VII of the Civil Rights Act of 1964.

*Bona fide occupational qualification (BFOQ) exception to federal employment discrimination law is determined on a case-by-case basis and can be allowed if one's religion, sex, national origin or age is an actual job qualification and/or the requirement is necessary to the employer's business.

Ban the Box

Ban the Box refers to the campaign started and led by American civil rights groups and advocates for ex-offenders, aimed at removing the check box that asks if applicants have a criminal record from hiring applications. Nationwide, 35 states and over 150 cities and counties have adopted Ban the Box.

To be clear, it doesn't stop you from running a background check, it encourages interviewers and employers to delay the focus on one's criminal history until after the interview process is complete. It leaves room for employers to consider the candidate's qualifications first—without the stigma of a conviction or arrest record.

Salary History Ban

The salary history ban prohibits employers (this includes hiring leaders, interviewers, and HR) from asking applicants and candidates about their current or past wages (including benefits). They generally also prohibit employers from obtaining this information through any third parties. If the applicant or candidate isn't comfortable offering this information, they cannot be forced to.

Avoid asking questions that either violate these laws directly or put your candidate in a position to provide information they aren't legally required to. You want to show that you're an informed employer who values the rights of their people. You show this by educating yourself and taking every step possible to respect their rights.

Part VIII

How Do I Welcome Someone into the Company?

(Offers & Onboarding)

Once you identify the right person, you need to think about how you're going to offer the job and how they're being brought onboard. This is important. This is your opportunity to welcome them to the team and start things off on the right foot.

Think about the process from their point of view. When presenting the offer, reach out and discuss the offer verbally, then follow up with a written offer. Give them a day or two (if needed) to think it over. Make sure that you aren't initiating any background checks or drug screens until they accept their offer.

Take the time to create an engaging onboarding experience. You want your new hire to be informed but also feel prepared and ready to begin their new job.

Make sure they have their equipment, access to their resources, and business cards on their first day. Create a welcome sign—this can be a physical sign or a digital one. Put it in a public area and show everyone (especially your new hire) how excited you are to have them onboard.

Arrange a new hire orientation for them to help them transition comfortably into the organization. The content and materials you share is ultimately up to you, but remember to look at the experience from their point of view.

If you have the staff size, think about pairing them up with a buddy to help them understand the culture and processes.

Think about some of the items below:

- What are the most important things I want all new hires to know about the organization?
- What is going to help them adjust and really feel at home here?
- What can I provide to help them along?
- What are the company policies and/or legal guidelines that protect them?

Quick Tip: You're going to have to think about this from different angles. It isn't just about company history, rules and regulations. You want your new hire to understand how important they are and be prepared for what they may experience. While it's impossible to anticipate and perfectly prepare for every single occurrence, you can make a new hire feel welcomed and at home on the first day.

Part IX

How do I plan for the Future?

(Training, Retention, & Succession Planning)

When someone accepts the offer to join your organization, they usually do so with plans for their future. You should have this in mind as well. Failing to think the process through in this way will cause you to lose the great people you hired.

If there is one word that describes this generation of job seekers, it's ambition! This generation of job seekers aren't satisfied with just having a 9-5. Many are launching podcasts, starting businesses, going back to school, and expecting promotions at a faster rate than their predecessors.

They want to be challenged.

They want to know that they'll be able to grow with your organization and have a real future there. Even if their title isn't changing, there may be a way to expand their role and allow for greater responsibility as the business grows. Growth can be many things.

Your new hire(s) wants to feel connected to their role(s) and the purpose behind the work they're doing. They want to understand their value. As an employer, you need to be prepared to communicate their value proposition from the interview and reinforce that after they're hired.

Think about the kind of future you want for your organization and how they'll fit in. Use that vision to shape, not only the current role, but future opportunities for your new hire(s).

Part X

How Do I Put This All Together?

(The Take-A-Ways & Dos and Don'ts of Hiring)

We've covered a lot so far, and if you're totally new to hiring, this may feel like information overload. Hiring isn't always a walk in the park, and there is much to consider. As an employer, you need to be clear on what your needs are, what the market looks like for you, what you can afford, and what's going to really work for you.

You want clarity around your vision for the role and the value you expect your new hire(s) to bring to your organization.

When hiring, there's much to consider. Here is where we bring it all together.

We're going to cover some important take-a-ways, best practices, as well as dos and don'ts.

1. Before you launch a search, take the time

needed to get clear on what your needs are now and what they will be in the foreseeable future.

2.   Remember that you're hiring a whole person. Make sure you're considering things like technical skills and education along with soft skills and culture fit.

3.   Make candidate experience a priority. Treat your candidates fairly. Respect their time and the courage it took for them to apply and interview for your role. They're people, and equally as important as you are.

4.   Put special emphasis on matching talent with your company's values and your management style. This will ensure a harmonious and productive working environment.

5.   Do your research. Know your market and understand your specific competitive landscape.

6.   Make sure that your budget will allow you to cover this person's salary, benefits, and any additional compensation allowed under their position and industry for a sufficient amount of time. You expect your business to grow, so think long term.

7.   Make sure you're clear on how you're going to evaluate your candidates and maintain

consistency throughout the process. Compliance is important each step of the way.

8.   Be honest with yourself and your candidates. Don't sugarcoat the challenges you're having as a company. You want someone to CHOOSE the opportunity in front of them, not be tricked into it. Being self-aware is critical to your success here. If you're unaware of your shortcomings as a leader, you will continue to struggle in hiring the right person to meet your needs.

9.   Making the offer and onboarding are key parts of the hiring process. The offer needs to cover each part of the role. Don't just focus on title and salary. Talk about benefits, perks, and any bonuses if you're offering them. If there is a background check, communicate that and agree on a start date. Send a written offer. This gives both you and your new hire a sense of security and confirms your agreement. With onboarding, you want to make sure your new hire receives a warm welcome into the organization and the team. You want them to feel at home.

10.   Set clear goals for your new hire. Check in regularly to make sure they're engaged, aware of their responsibilities, and know the expectations around their role. Be open to their questions, ideas, and concerns. Hear their challenges and partner with them to identify real solutions. Don't just delegate and dictate. Lead.

This is how you hire.

The Dos and Don'ts You Need to Remember

DO remember that you're hiring a complete person and not just a résumé.

When you're evaluating applicants, remember that a person is more than just their resume. When interviewing candidates, look for more than just technical skills, educational background, industry knowledge, and years of experience. Pay attention to things like attitude and look for opportunities to learn more about their work ethic and integrity.

Did your candidate say something during the interview that resonated with you on an emotional and philosophical level? Did they make you laugh? Can you envision yourself working well with them every day? These are all signs of someone being a "good fit" with an organization, and are things one cannot learn in a classroom.

DO employ creative sourcing methods.

Employers have options when it comes to sourcing talent. You can use social media, tap into your network or the networks of those you know, you can solicit employee referrals, or post your need publicly.

You have many choices but that doesn't mean you can't get creative.

One thing I've learned after years in recruitment is this: you can find a great candidate anywhere. Honestly, you can find great talent ANYWHERE.

You can meet amazing candidates while running errands, having dinner with a friend, or on the way to the office. You have to be open to meeting and connecting with people.

Have a conversation with the person next to you on the plane or in the elevator. Make the effort to go where you might find the people you'd want to hire. If you're trying to hire an Executive Chef, start eating out more. Go to different types of restaurants. Read the entire menu before ordering. Pay special attention to the food quality and level of service. If you like what you see, ask to meet the chef, then slip them a business card.

Hiring can be an enjoyable experience if you're willing to get creative and do something new.

DO tell the truth.

While it is important to make an opportunity as attractive as possible, it is equally important that you are honest with your candidates. Without honesty in the hiring process, you rob your candidate of their right to make an informed decision that will impact theirs and their family's lives.

If the hours are long, say so.

Be frank about the cultural challenges and opportunities for improvement. Don't deny, try to hide, or beat around the bush about them. Forget the sales pitch. Be transparent.

DO remember that your candidate is also your customer.
Even if you aren't planning to hire them, it's important they have a positive experience while interviewing. Be kind and respect their time. Employees and candidates regularly share their experiences and feedback online for all to see. The feedback provided influences how employers are viewed in the marketplace. They shape your reputation; directly impacting employer brand and your ability to recruit the kind of talent your business needs.

DO maintain consistency throughout the process.

If you're using any kind of pre-qualifying questions, standard interview questions, or assessments, maintain consistency as you go from candidate to candidate. You want to have as much of an "apples to apples" comparison as possible. This will help you come to the best decision and ensure everyone has a similar experience.

DO remember that time is of the essence.

Job seekers are most attracted to new job ads and may shy away from older ones thinking that the job may be filled already or may not be a critical need. When you launch a search, you want to move on applicants quickly and avoid passing the 30 day mark.

DO make sure your questions and overall process connect directly to the job.

Think carefully about what you're asking in the interview. Be mindful of the kinds of assessments you're using. Make sure this is all directly relevant to the job itself. If it isn't, you won't be able to verify that you're truly hiring the right person (or people) for the role. (For example: If the job doesn't require one to sell anything, then they shouldn't be evaluated on their ability to sell.)

DO choose potential over perfection.

There is no such thing as the perfect job seeker just like there is no such thing as the perfect company. If you're waiting for perfection, you might as well cancel your search. What you want is potential. Do you know why?

Potential is hungry. Potential asks great questions

and wants to learn. Potential appreciates you taking a chance on them and are making as big of an investment as you are. Someone with potential will grow with your organization and continue to add value over time.

If you find that you're struggling to identify someone with 100% of what you're looking for, try hiring someone with 80% and training the rest. Be open minded. You just might find that diamond in the rough you need.

DO remember the applicable employment laws.
Make sure your application isn't asking for any information that violates a job seeker's rights. If you have existing forms, take this time to review them. Making sure they're compliant with the latest employment laws. For example, applicants aren't required to provide their social security numbers or date of birth when applying. This is only necessary when an offer has gone out and a background check is being performed.

When interviewing, avoid any questions that invades someone's privacy, opens the door to discrimination or bias. The interview sets the tone for the working relationship. If one feels discriminated against in the interview process, what will they expect should they decide to work for you? Show your candidates that you run a respectful, non-discriminatory, and legally compliant workplace. Show them that as potential employees they can expect to be treated with dignity.

DON'T move forward without a plan.

Have you ever heard that those who fail to plan, plan to fail? Well, the same goes for your interview strategy. Before you schedule one interview, you need to have a plan!

This ensures consistency, integrity, and validity in the process. It ensures that you have a true "apples to apples" comparison and can truly rely on the results you get from the interviews. You'll want to have clearly defined standards and know that you're making the best decision for your business.
This is important.

DON'T feel like you have to interview every applicant.

Their application should make you want to interview them. When you read their resume, you should be excited to meet with them. If you aren't, simply move on to the next applicant. There's nothing wrong with that. Many candidates would prefer you move on instead of pretending to be interested in them. No one wants to be the charity case. If you know by the resume and application that it isn't a fit, feel comfortable moving on. There's no sense in wasting their time or yours.

DON'T make your candidate jump through any unnecessary hoops.

Resist the temptation to use irrelevant assessments or 10 rounds of interviews in an attempt to get your candidate to prove they really want the job. Treat your candidates the way you'd want to be treated. Use the tools and information in this book to create an interview strategy that allows you to properly screen your candidates in a fair amount of time.

Anything else can come off as annoying, and in the long run, will turn people off. Candidate experience is everything. You don't want people quitting on you before they've started.

DON'T post a job without EEO (Equal Employment Opportunity) verbiage.

It's important to show that you are a fair and unbiased employer who is looking for the most qualified person regardless of race, gender, religion, disability, etc.

Adding one or two sentences at the end of your job ad (you can ask your HR lead or find examples online) can greatly impact how your job posting and company are perceived.

DON'T extend an offer prematurely.

The hiring process, believe it or not, is an emotional one. While we have key skills areas we focus on, and a host of tools to help us make the best decisions, hiring leaders hire the candidate they'd most like to work with. This includes someone who is skilled but also someone who is a cultural fit. When we find that person who is a strong cultural fit, it can be tempting to shout, "You're hired!" Don't fall into that temptation. Make the effort to meet with a few different people. You don't need to interview 50 people, but you certainly want to interview more than one.

Do your best to meet with a diverse group of candidates and resist the urge to hire someone because they remind you of yourself. Remember that a company doesn't grow by hiring the same people over and over. Just as the body needs different parts working together to function, your organization needs different types of people working together to be successful.

DON'T forget to leave room for your candidate's questions.

An interview isn't one sided. As an organization, you're being interviewed as well. If your interview is expected to last an hour, try to keep your portion of the conversation to 45 minutes and end by asking, "Do you have any questions for me?" Be sure that you are kind and sincere when responding as well.

A candidate's questions tell you a lot about who they are. If they have no questions, at any point in the interview, it could mean that they aren't as interested as they seem. It could also mean that they weren't really paying attention and have already forgotten most of what you said. No questions is not a good sign, so leave room for this.

Conclusion

Hiring is matchmaking. Pure and simple. You want to be sure that the person (or people) you're hiring fit with the job(s), your organization, the team, and you. Enjoy the process of meeting talented people, building great relationships, adding value to your organization, and seeing your business grow.

Don't chase perfection. Chase integrity and a positive attitude. Hire the brilliant candidate who has the unique qualities you can't teach, and put effort into training the rest.

Invest the time and resources necessary to create a warm and welcoming onboarding experience. Show your new hire that you're happy they accepted your offer. Stay on top of employment trends, applicable laws, and best practices. All of this will help ensure you hire the right kind of talent for your business and create an environment in which they can flourish. Remember that when your people do well, your business does well.

Happy hiring!

References

Steiner, Keenan. "Bad Candidate Experience Cost Virgin Media $5M Annually – Here is How They Turned That Around." LinkedIn Talent Blog, March 15, 2017. https://business.linkedin.com/talent-solutions/blog/candidate-experience/2017/bad-candidate-experience-cost-virgin-media-5m-annually-and-how-they-turned-that-around.

The Hire Team. "Great Candidate Experience Isn't a 'Nice to Have'—It Cuts Costs and Drives Revenue." Hire by Google. Google, September 19, 2018. https://hire.google.com/articles/great-candidate-experience/.

Richards, Tressa Sloane. "A Lesson on How the Candidate Experience Is Tied to Business Revenue." Rally® Recruitment Marketing. Rally, June 27, 2019. https://rallyrecruitmentmarketing.com/2019/06/a-lesson-on-how-the-candidate-experience-is-tied-to-business-revenue/.

About the Author

Pamela Shand is a sought-after HR leader, career coach, resume writer, trainer, and job search expert. Pamela grew up in Englewood, New Jersey. The daughter of Costa Rican and Jamaican, descent, her parents instilled in her the importance of a strong work ethic, ambition, and perseverance.

She started her career in talent acquisition nearly 15 years ago working with Fortune 500 heavyweights Goldman Sachs, Merrill Lynch, and MetLife. Pamela began using what she learned to help those around her improve their job searches and get better-paying opportunities. The advice and tools she provided to family and friends worked! Word of mouth spread and soon she had no choice but to launch Offer Stage Consulting, LLC in 2016. Today, Offer Stage now partners with career professionals at all levels, growing companies, and educators to inspire, motivate, disrupt, and transform.

Pamela has a BA in Public Administration (Kean University), an MS in HR Management (New York Institute of Technology), and is a certified professional resume writer (CPRW) by the Professional Association of Resume Writers and Career Coaches (PARW/CC).

Linkedin.com/company/offerstage
Facebook: Facebook.com/offerstage
Instagram: Instagram.com/offerstage
Twitter: Twitter.com/offerstage

www.ingramcontent.com/pod-product-compliance
Lightning Source LLC
Chambersburg PA
CBHW020437220526
45464CB00002B/746